SPIRITUAL ADVICE

SPIRITUAL ADVICE *from*

THE SAINTS

365 DAYS OF INSPIRATION

Compiled by
Daughters of St. Paul

BOOKS & MEDIA
Boston

ISBN 08198-7085-4

Cover photos: FSP Photo Archives

Published in the U.S.A. by Pauline Books & Media, 50 Saint Pauls Avenue, Boston, MA 02130-3491.

Printed in Korea.

"P" and PAULINE are registered trademarks of the Daughters of St. Paul

www.pauline.org

Pauline Books & Media is the publishing house of the Daughters of St. Paul, an international congregation of women religious serving the Church with the communications media.

2 3 4 5 6 7 8   11 10 09 08 07 06 05

Introduction

Along the path of life, nothing so consoles and strengthens the human heart as the companionship of trusted friends. And what truer expression of friendship could there be than a sincere interest in our spiritual well-being? Such is the concern shown for us by the saints through their counsels. In these men and women we discover friends who, from their own experience, understand profoundly the struggles, doubts, fears, and difficulties we encounter in living our Christian vocation to holiness.

Spiritual Advice from the Saints contains a wealth of insight and encouragement for our pilgrimage, for "when we look at the lives of those who have faithfully followed Christ, we are inspired with a new reason for seeking the city that is to come (cf. Heb 13:14; 11:10), and at the same time we are shown a most safe path by which among the vicissitudes of this world...we will be able to arrive at perfect union with Christ, that is, perfect holiness" (*Lumen Gentium,* no. 50).

With this volume, we can take hold of the bright threads of Christian wisdom from the saints and weave them into the fabric of our own way of discipleship, sharing with these great witnesses that seamless garment of the Church on earth and in heaven.

January

*C*onsider every day
that you are for the first time, as it were,
beginning anew; and always act with the
same fervor as on the first day you began.

Saint Anthony of Padua

January 1

*Y*ou are to be radiant lights as you stand beside Christ, the great light, bathed in the glory of him who is the light.

Saint Gregory of Nazianzen

*T*he value of life does not depend upon the place we occupy. It depends upon the way we occupy that place.

Saint Thérèse of Lisieux

January 3

January 4

*I*n every disappoinment,
great or small, let your heart fly directly
to your dear Savior, throwing yourself
into those arms for refuge against every
pain and sorrow. Jesus will never leave
you or forsake you.

Saint Elizabeth Ann Seton

*O*pen your compassion to all God's disciples. Don't be put off by appearance or age. Don't fret about those who seem to be penniless, ragged, ugly, or feeble and turn away from them. For hidden within their human form dwells the Father and the Son, who died for us and rose with us.

Saint Clement of Alexandria

January 5

*I*nterior silence—
the inner stillness to which meditation
leads—is where the Spirit secretly anoints
the soul and heals our deepest wounds.

Saint John of the Cross

*A*cquire the habit of speaking to God as if you were alone with God. Speak with familiarity and confidence as to your dearest and most loving friend. Speak of your life, your plans, your troubles, your joys, your fears. In return, God will speak to you—not that you will hear audible words in your ears, but words that you will clearly understand in your heart.

Saint Alphonsus Liguori

January 7

*N*ow that we are reborn...in the likeness of our Lord, and have indeed been adopted by God as his children, let us put on the complete image of our Creator so as to be wholly like him ...in innocence, simplicity, gentleness, patience, humility, mercy, harmony; those qualities in which he chose to become, and to be, one with us.

Saint Peter Chrysologus

$\mathcal{I}$t is so beautiful to be poor, to have nothing, to wait simply on the good God.

Blessed Jeanne Jugan

January 9

No one can be happy unless that person rise above himself or herself, not by an ascent of the body, but of the heart. But we cannot rise above ourselves unless a higher power lifts us up. And divine aid is available to those who seek it from their hearts, humbly and devoutly.

Saint Bonaventure

*T*he Son of God desires
to perfect the mystery of his Incarnation
and birth by forming himself in us and
being reborn in our souls through the
blessed sacraments of Baptism and
Eucharist. He fulfills his hidden life in us,
hidden with him in God.

Saint John Eudes

January 11

January 12

*O*ur life is sown with tiny thorns that produce in our hearts a thousand involuntary movements of hatred, envy, fear, impatience..., a thousand disturbances that momentarily alter our peace of soul. For example, a word escapes that should not have been spoken. Or someone utters another that offends you. A child inconveniences you.... You don't like the weather. Your work is not going according to plan....

I know that these are not occasions for practicing very heroic virtue, but they would definitely be enough to acquire it if we really wished to.

Saint Claude de la Colombière

$\mathcal{W}$e who have been reborn through the sacrament of Baptism experience intense joy when we feel within us the first stirrings of the Holy Spirit.... We become steadfast in hope and receive the gift of healing.... These gifts enter us like a gentle rain, and, once having done so, little by little they bring forth fruit in abundance.

Saint Hilary

January 13

January 14

O Lord Jesus, I surren-
der to you all my will. Let me be your
lute. Touch any string you please. Always
and forever let me make music in perfect
harmony with your own. Yes, Lord, with
no ifs, ands, or buts, let your will be done
in this family...for everything that con-
cerns us, and especially let your will be
done in me.

Saint Jane Frances de Chantal

$\mathcal{Y}$ou will never know
real mercy for the failings of others until
you know and realize that you have the
same failings.

Saint Bernard of Clairvaux

January 15

January 16

*O*ur Lord and Savior
lifted up his voice and said with incom-
parable majesty: "Let all know that grace
comes after tribulation. Let them know
that without the burden of afflictions it is
impossible to reach the height of grace.
Let them know that the gifts of grace
increase as the struggles increase."

Saint Rose of Lima

*T*he trouble is that everyone talks about reforming others, and no one thinks about reforming himself.

Saint Peter of Alcantara

January 17

January 18

*G*rant me the grace to
spend this day without offending you and
without failing my neighbor.

Saint Louise de Marillac

$\mathcal{L}$et us make in ourselves a dwelling wholly at peace, in
which is always sung the canticle of love
and gratitude followed by silence, an
echo of the very silence of God.

Blessed Elizabeth of the Trinity

January 19

January 20

*S*hould we fall into sin, let us humble ourselves sorrowfully in God's presence. Then, with an act of unbounded confidence, let us throw ourselves into the ocean of his goodness, where every failing will be cancelled and every anxiety turned into love.

Saint Paul of the Cross

*W*e must have a real living determination to reach holiness. "I will be a saint" means I will despoil myself of all that is not God; I will strip my heart of all created things; I will live in poverty and detachment; I will renounce my will, my inclinations, my whims and fancies, and make myself a willing slave to the will of God.

Blessed Teresa of Calcutta

January 21

*T*here is no time of life
past learning something.

Saint Ambrose

Go not outside, return into yourself; the truth dwells in the inner person.

Saint Augustine of Hippo

January 23

January 24

*T*hose people are truly peacemakers who, regardless of what they suffer in this world, maintain peace of spirit and body, because of love of our Lord Jesus Christ.

Saint Francis of Assisi

*T*he true personality is one that is rooted in Christ; that is, a personality in which our thoughts are conformed to the thoughts of Jesus: we think like Jesus, love what Jesus loves, desire and do what Jesus would desire and do.

Blessed James Alberione

January 25

January 26

*T*he first degree of
humility is obedience without delay.

Saint Benedict

*T*he only way to make rapid progress along the path of divine love is to remain very little and to put all our trust in Almighty God. That is what I have done.

Saint Thérèse of Lisieux

January 27

January 28

*B*oth the light of rea-
son and the light of faith come from God.
Therefore there can be no contradiction
between them.

                              Saint Thomas Aquinas

$\mathcal{D}$o something good
for someone you like least today.

Saint Anthony of Padua

January 29

January 30

I saw that God is to us everything that is good and comfortable for us. He is our clothing which for love enwraps us, holds us, and all encloses us because of his tender love, so that he may never leave us.

Blessed Julian of Norwich

$\mathcal{I}$n serious matters it is better to beg God humbly than to send forth a flood of words that will only offend the listeners and have no effect on those who are guilty.

Saint John Bosco

January 31

February

$\mathcal{I}$f I love you, Lord, it is not just because of heaven, which you have promised; if I fear to offend you, it is not because hell threatens me. What draws me to you, O Lord, is yourself alone.... Your love so holds my heart that, if there were no heaven, I would love you still.

Saint Teresa of Avila

February 1

*T*he Mother of God, the most pure Virgin, carried the true light in her arms and brought him to those who lay in darkness. We, too, should carry a light for all to see and reflect the radiance of the true light as we hasten to meet him.

Saint Sophronius

*H*atred is not a creative force; only love is a creative power.

Saint Maximilian Kolbe

February 3

February 4

*W*e do not say my
Father, but our Father, neither do we say
give me, but give us. The Teacher of
unity did not wish...that each should pray
for oneself alone.

Saint Cyprian

$\mathcal{W}$ell and good if all things change, Lord God, provided we are rooted in you.

Saint John of the Cross

February 5

February 6

*A*sk Christ to help
you to become happy.

Saint Paul Miki

$\mathcal{I}$ will abandon myself fully to the Holy Spirit, allowing myself to be led wherever and whenever the Spirit wants, accompanying the Spirit, for my part, with effective and strong resolutions and serious discernment.... The Holy Spirit descends upon us with great gentleness, never with a racket.

Saint Frances Xavier Cabrini

February 7

*E*ternal life is a canticle of adoration, of thanksgiving, of reparation, of love. We must begin here below to do what we will be doing for all eternity.

Blessed Timothy Giaccardo

*T*he more perfectly and purely we see, the more perfectly and purely we love. As we see, so we love. Therefore, the more we see of Jesus Christ, God and man, the more we are transformed into him by love.

Blessed Angela of Foligno

February 9

February 10

*O*ne who can preserve
gentleness amid pains, and peace amid
worry and a multitude of affairs, is
almost perfect.

Saint Francis de Sales

*A*ssist me, my Jesus, for I desire to become good whatsoever it may cost. Take away, destroy, and utterly root out all that you find in me contrary to your holy will. At the same time, I pray you, Lord Jesus, to enlighten me that I may be able to walk in your holy light.

Saint Gemma Galgani

February 11

February 12

*T*hose who want to
understand the unfathomable depths of
God must first consider the world of
nature. Knowledge of the Trinity is rightly
compared with the depths of the sea....
As the depths of the sea are invisible to
human sight, so the godhead of the
Trinity is found to be beyond the grasp of
human understanding.

Saint Columban

*T*his is our lot: to
rejoice in study and work. This is a good
goal, but not completely good until Christ
is revealed in our lives.

Saint Jerome

February 13

*V*irtue is nothing but well-directed love.

Saint Augustine of Hippo

$\mathcal{M}$y Good
Shepherd, who have shown your very
gentle mercy to us unworthy sinners in
various physical pains and sufferings,
give grace and strength to me, your little
lamb, that in no tribulation or anguish or
pain may I turn away from you.

Saint Francis of Assisi

February 15

February 16

Humanity, there is nothing left for you to boast of, for your boasting and hope lie in putting to death all that is your own and seeking the future life that is in Christ. Since we have its first fruits, we are already in its midst, living entirely in the grace and gift of God.

Saint Basil the Great

*T*he patient and humble endurance of the cross—whatever nature it may be—is the highest work we have to do.

Saint Katharine Drexel

February 17

February **18**

*T*he harvest is good,
and one reaper or even several would not
suffice to gather all of it into the granary
of the Lord.

Saint Thomas Becket

*D*uring painful times, when you feel a terrible void, think how God is enlarging the capacity of your soul so that it can receive him—making it, as it were, infinite as he is infinite. Look upon each pain as a love token coming to you directly from God in order to unite you to him.

Blessed Elizabeth of the Trinity

February **19**

*C*hristians must lean on the cross of Christ just as travelers lean on a staff when they begin a long journey. They must have the passion of Christ deeply imbedded in their minds and hearts, because only from it can they derive peace, grace, and truth.

Saint Anthony of Padua

*L*et the serenity of your spirit shine through your face. Let the joy of your mind burst forth. Let words of thanks break from your lips.

Saint Peter Damian

February 21

February 22

*S*implicity is the precise aiming of one's thought toward the goal one wants to reach. It is the measure of the time available—however much is needed for the instruction of the faithful and not for the pleasure of listening to oneself....

Blessed John XXIII

*H*elp one another with the generosity of the Lord, and despise no one. When you have the opportunity to do good, do not let it go by.

Saint Polycarp

February 23

February 24

I have always been
taught that the secret of happiness is living moment by moment and to thank
God for everything that he sends us in
his goodness, day after day.

Saint Gianna Beretta Molla

*R*emember that the Christian life is one of action, not of speech and daydreams. Let there be few words and many deeds, and let them be done well.

Saint Vincent Pallotti

February 25

February 26

*B*eauty and the
enchantment of life pass away; there
remains alone eternal love surviving in
us, which is our hope and religion, for
God is love. The grandeur of death is not
the end, but the beginning of the sublime
and the Divine, in whose presence flowers and beauty are as nothing.

Saint Joseph Moscati

$\mathcal{I}$t is here...that love is
to be found: not hidden away in corners
but in the midst of the occasions of sin.
And believe me, although we may more
often fail and commit small lapses, our
gain will be incomparably the greater.

Saint Teresa of Avila

February 27

February 28

If you say, "Show me your God," I will say to you, "Show me what kind of person you are, and I will show you my God." Show me then whether the eyes of your mind can see, and the ears of your heart hear.

Saint Theophilus of Antioch

March

*W*hen the love of Jesus is in question, let our generosity know no bounds; we can never bear enough for the God who suffered so much for us.

Saint Madeleine Sophie Barat

March 1

*G*od places more value on good will in all we do than on the works themselves. Therefore, whether we give ourselves to God in the work of contemplation or whether we serve the needs of our neighbor by good works, we accomplish these things because the love of Christ urges us on.

Saint Lawrence Justinian

*E*verything passes away! At the end of life, love alone remains.... We must do everything by love; we must forget ourselves at all times. The good God so loves for us to forget ourselves....

Blessed Elizabeth of the Trinity

March 3

$\mathcal{E}$ven though the poor are often rough and unrefined, we must not judge them from external appearances.... If you consider the poor in the light of faith, then you will observe that they are taking the place of the Son of God, who chose to be poor.

Saint Vincent de Paul

*L*et us spread before [Christ's] feet, not garments or soulless olive branches, which delight the eye for a few hours and then wither, but ourselves, clothed in his grace, or rather, clothed completely in him. We who have been baptized into Christ must ourselves be the garments that we spread before him.

Saint Andrew of Crete

March 5

*G*od embraces with incomprehensible love the soul who lives by his will. I understood how much God loves us, how simple he is, though incomprehensible, and how easy it is to commune with him, despite his great majesty. With no one do I feel as free and as much at ease as with him.

Saint Faustina Kowalska

*I*nstead of measuring your difficulties with your strength, you must measure them with the powerful help you have a right to expect from God.

Saint Elizabeth Ann Seton

March 7

March 8

*I*f we look forward to
receiving God's mercy, we can never fail to
do good so long as we have the strength.
For if we share with the poor, out of love
for God, whatever he has given to us, we
shall receive according to his promise a
hundredfold in eternal happiness. What a
fine profit, what a blessed reward!

Saint John of God

*L*et us remember that the life in which we ought to be interested is "daily" life. We can, each of us, call only the present time our own.

Saint Gregory of Nyssa

March 9

March 10

*D*o not desire crosses,
unless you have borne well those laid on
you; it is an abuse to long after martyrdom while being unable to bear an insult
patiently.

Saint Francis de Sales

*D*o not say: it is impossible for me to influence others. If you are a Christian, it is impossible for this not to happen.

Saint John Chrysostom

March 11

*D*o not destroy the
whole Christ by separating head from
body, for Christ is not complete without
the Church, nor is the Church complete
without Christ.

Blessed Isaac of Stella

$\mathcal{E}$ducation is something from the heart, and God alone is its master; we cannot succeed in anything unless God gives us the key to these [children's] hearts.

Saint John Bosco

March 13

*I*f you say: "I can't climb this tree; it's too high," I answer that [Christ] has hollowed out steps for you in his body. First raise yourself, heart and soul, to the feet of God's Son; then climb up to the heart, which is open and utterly spent for us.

Saint Catherine of Siena

*W*e are greatly deceiv-
ing ourselves if we think that we are
capable of great perfection, and even more
so if we believe that we can attain such
perfection by our own efforts and by con-
stantly and closely watching over all the
movements and dispositions of our souls.

Saint Louise de Marillac

March 15

*A*ll who undertake
to teach must be endowed with deep love,
the greatest patience, and, most of all,
profound humility.

Saint Joseph Calasanz

Christ with me, Christ before me,
Christ behind me, Christ within me,
Christ beneath me, Christ above me,
Christ at my right, Christ at my left,
Christ in my lying down,
Christ in my sitting,
Christ in my arising.
Christ in the heart of everyone who
  thinks of me,
Christ in the mouth of everyone
  who speaks to me,
Christ in every eye that sees me,
Christ in every ear that hears me.

Saint Patrick

March 17

March 18

*W*e must always correspond to the grace of God to the best of our ability, not through fear of sin, but from a sentiment of love.

Blessed Mother Theodore Guerin

*G*rant me to impart
willingly to others whatever I possess
that is good, and to ask humbly of others
that I may partake of the good of which I
am destitute....

Saint Thomas Aquinas

March **19**

March 20

*C*hrist has no body now on earth but yours; no hands but yours, no feet but yours. Yours are the eyes through which Christ's compassion is to look out on the world. Yours are the feet with which he is to go about doing good. Yours are the hands with which he is to bless men and women now.

Saint Teresa of Avila

*W*e do not really belong to ourselves; we belong to the One who redeemed us. Our will should always depend on this.

Saint Braulio

March 21

*W*hen the stomach is
full, it is easy to talk of fasting.

Saint John Mary Vianney

*S*avior, your crucifixion marked the end of your mortal life; teach us to crucify ourselves and make way for our life in the Spirit. May your resurrection, Jesus, bring true greatness to our spiritual self, and may your sacraments be the mirror wherein we may know that self.

Saint Ephrem

March 23

*P*ray and make others pray so that God will not abandon his Church, but will reform it as he wills and as he sees best for us and for his greater glory.

Saint Angela Merici

*A*dmire both the benign condescension of the Son and the most excellent dignity of the Mother, and choose which one of the two is the more admirable. Each is a wonder, each a miracle. God is obedient to a woman, an unexampled humility! A woman is in the place of ancestor to God, a distinction without match.

Saint Bernard of Clairvaux

March 25

*G*od is faithful, and if
we serve him faithfully, he will provide
for our needs.

Saint Richard of Chichester

*T*he truest crosses are
those we do not choose ourselves.

Saint Rose Philippine Duchesne

March 27

*L*et us preach the whole of God's plan to the powerful and to the humble, to rich and to poor, to those of every rank and age, as far as God gives us the strength, in season and out of season....

Saint Boniface

$\mathcal{I}$t is very good and holy to consider the passion of our Lord and to meditate on it, for by this sacred path we reach union with God. In this most holy school we learn true wisdom, for it was there that all the saints learned it.

Saint Paul of the Cross

March 29

*J*ust as you see that a ray of light entering through a window is colored in different ways according to the different colors of the various parts, so the divine ray shines forth in each and every creature in different ways and in different properties.

Saint Bonaventure

*Y*ou are the fire which takes away cold; with your light you illuminate me so that I may know all your truth. Clothe me, clothe me with yourself, eternal truth, so that I may run this mortal life with true obedience, and with the light of your most holy faith.

Saint Catherine of Siena

March 31

April

$\mathscr{W}$e were deceived by
the wisdom of the serpent, but we are
freed by the foolishness of God.

Saint Augustine of Hippo

April 1

April 2

Take pains to refrain from sharp words. If they escape your lips, do not be ashamed to let your lips produce the remedy, since they have caused the wounds.

Saint Francis of Paola

*A*h! Do let us stay very far from all that is brilliant. Let us love our littleness, love to feel nothing; then we shall be poor in spirit—and Jesus will come for us, far off as we are. He will transform us....

Saint Thérèse of Lisieux

April 3

April 4

*D*own with all melancholy. That should never find a place except in the heart which has lost faith. I am joyful. Sorrow is not gloom. Gloom should be banished from the Christian soul.

Blessed Pier Giorgio Frassati

$\mathcal{I}$f you truly want to help the soul of your neighbor, you should approach God first with all your heart.

Saint Vincent Ferrer

April 5

O Christ Jesus, may
your death be my life, your labor my
repose, your human weakness my
strength, your confusion my glory.

Blessed Peter Faber

$\mathcal{L}$et us not disturb the design in which God calls everyone to cooperate, weaving the threads of a fabric that will be completed with his grace and with the ready service of innocent, meek, and generous souls.

Blessed John XXIII

April 7

*H*oliness is not a luxury for the few; it is not just for some people. It is meant for you and for me and for all of us. It is a simple duty, because if we learn to love, we learn to be holy.

Blessed Teresa of Calcutta

$\mathcal{W}$e shall be blessed with clear vision if we keep our eyes fixed on Christ. As no darkness can be seen by anyone surrounded by light, so no trivialities can capture the attention of one who has his eyes on Christ.

Saint Gregory of Nyssa

April 9

April 10

*A*s by his courtesy
God forgives our sins when we repent,
even so he wills that we should forgive
our sins, and so give up our senseless
worrying and faithless fear.

Blessed Julian of Norwich

*T*he Divine Master must reign over all, must be given integrally to everyone: to form their minds with his Gospel, their wills and habits with his holiness, their hearts with his heart, their bodies with his cross, their spirits and lives with his prayer and with the Eucharist....

Blessed Timothy Giaccardo

April 11

April 12

*W*e should live like the
temples of God we are, so that it can be
seen that God lives in us. No act of ours
should be unworthy of the Spirit.

Saint Cyprian

*C*hrist did not say: "Learn from me to fast," although he fasted forty days and forty nights. He did not say: "Learn from me to despise the world and to live in poverty," although he lived in very great poverty and wished that his disciples live in the same way. He did not say: "Learn from me to perform miracles," although he himself performed miracles by his own power and wished that his disciples do so in his name. But he said simply: "Learn from me, because I am meek and humble of heart."

Blessed Angela of Foligno

April 13

April 14

*S*ettle yourself in solitude and you will come upon God in yourself.

Saint Teresa of Avila

*W*hat a joy it is to serve God freely, generously, without asking recompense!

Saint Rose Philippine Duchesne

April 15

*G*od made us without
ourselves, but he will not save us without
ourselves.

Saint Augustine of Hippo

One prays best who
does not know he is praying.

Saint Anthony of Egypt

April 17

April **18**

$\mathcal{I}$ would not consider
any spirituality worthwhile that wants to
walk in sweetness and ease and run from
the imitation of Christ.

Saint John Climacus

*T*o offer ourselves to the Father; to fulfill his adorable will—this is the path of holiness as I understand it.

Saint Teresa of the Andes

April 19

April 20

*T*he language that God
hears best is the silent language of love.

Saint John of the Cross

*E*nter into your mind's inner chamber. Shut out everything but God and whatever helps you to seek him; and when you have shut the door, look for him.

Saint Anselm

April 21

April 22

I have lived for Christ. I want to die for Christ.

Blessed Restituta Kafka

*W*hy...are you so worthless in your own eyes and yet so precious to God? Why render yourself such dishonor when you are honored by him? ...It was for you that the light dispelled the overshadowing gloom; for your sake was the night regulated and the day measured, and for you were the heavens embellished with the varying brilliance of the sun, the moon, and the stars. ...And the Creator still works to devise things that can add to your glory.

Saint Peter Chrysologus

April 23

April 24

*T*he death of the mar-
tyrs blossoms in the faith of the living.
Saint Fidelis of Sigmaringen

*W*e have received
Baptism, entrance into the Church, and
the honor of being called Christians. Yet
what good will this do us if we are
Christians in name only and not in fact?

Saint Andrew Kim

April 25

*W*e need to find God,
and he cannot be found in noise and
restlessness. God is the friend of silence.

Blessed Teresa of Calcutta

When you are unable to take big steps on the path along which God leads you, patiently wait until your legs are strong enough to run, or rather, until you have the wings to fly.

Saint Pio of Pietrelcina

April 27

*M*ary's chief pur-
pose is to unite us with Jesus Christ, her
Son; and it is the most decided wish of
her Son that we should come to him
through his Blessed Mother.

Saint Louis de Montfort

*E*ternal Trinity, Godhead, mystery deep as the sea, you could give me no greater gift than the gift of yourself. For you are a fire ever burning and never consumed, which itself consumes all the selfish love that fills my being.

Saint Catherine of Siena

April 29

April 30

$\mathcal{I}$ngratitude is the soul's
enemy; it empties it of merit, scatters its
virtues, and deprives it of graces.

Saint Bernard of Clairvaux

May

A tree is known by its fruit; a person by her deeds. A good deed is never lost; one who sows courtesy reaps friendship, and one who plants kindness gathers love.

Saint Basil

May **1**

*C*hrist is not complete by himself; he is complete when he lives in us—that is, Christ "plus" us make up Jesus Christ's Mystical Body.

Blessed James Alberione

*L*ove is not to be pur-
chased, and affection has no price.

Saint Jerome

May 3

May 4

*W*e must not wish anything other than what happens from moment to moment, all the while, however, exercising ourselves in goodness.

Saint Catherine of Genoa

*T*rue humility scarcely
ever utters words of humility.

Saint Francis de Sales

May 5

*C*ountless numbers are deceived in multiplying prayers. I would rather say five words devoutly and with my heart than five thousand which my soul does not relish with affection and understanding.

Saint Edmund the Martyr

*E*ternity—oh, how near it seems to me now!... Oh, that we may spend it in praising, blessing, and adoring forever.

Saint Elizabeth Ann Seton

May 7

May 8

*I*f you desire to praise
God, then live what you express. Live
good lives, and you yourself will be God's
praise.

Saint Augustine of Hippo

*E*very vocation is a
vocation to the material, spiritual, and
moral motherhood, and to prepare oneself
to be a donor of life.

Saint Gianna Beretta Molla

May 9

May 10

*T*he cross will not
crush you; if its weight makes you stag-
ger, its power will also sustain you.

Saint Pio of Pietrelcina

*Y*ou are one with Jesus
as the body is one with the head. You
must, then, have one breath with him,
one soul, one life, one will, one heart.
And he must be your breath, heart, love,
life, your all. These great gifts in the fol-
lower of Christ originate from Baptism.
They are increased and strengthened
through Confirmation and by making
good use of other graces that are given
by God. Through the Holy Eucharist they
are brought to perfection.

Saint John Eudes

May 11

May 12

*T*here is no more
excellent way to obtain graces from God
than to seek them through Mary, because
her divine Son cannot refuse her anything.

Saint Philip Neri

*M*ay it please the
supreme and divine Goodness to give us
all abundant grace ever to know his most
holy will and perfectly to fulfill it.

Saint Ignatius of Loyola

May 13

$\mathcal{I}$t is God's will that we should rejoice with him in our salvation, and that we should be cheered and strengthened by it. He wants our soul to delight in its salvation, through his grace. For we are the apple of his eye.

Blessed Julian of Norwich

$\mathcal{Y}$ou learn to speak by speaking, to study by studying, to run by running, to work by working. In just the same way, you learn to love by loving.

Saint Francis de Sales

May 15

*L*ove the Immaculata, love the Immaculata, love the Immaculata! Confide in her. Consecrate yourself to her entirely and without reserve. I wish you to love her so much as to be incapable of living without her.

Saint Maximilian Kolbe

*A*ll those who observe the ways of the good God are led to believe that God wants something. When and how? That is the mystery I am willing to adore!

Saint Julie Billiart

May 17

May 18

*H*elp me, O my God;
help me to conquer myself! This I ask
through your infinite mercy. To obtain it,
I offer you the merits of Jesus Christ, our
Savior and Lord. I have no merits of my
own; I am destitute, but his wounds will
be my plea.

Saint Gabriel of the Sorrowful Mother

No one heals himself
by wounding another.

Saint Ambrose

May 19

May 20

*W*henever the divine favor chooses someone to receive a special grace or to accept a lofty vocation, God adorns the person chosen with all the gifts of the Spirit needed to fulfill the task at hand.

Saint Bernardine of Siena

O Jesus, I love you
very much.... Tell me what you wish me
to do, and do with me as you will.

Saint Frances Xavier Cabrini

May 21

May 22

*B*e not anxious about
what you have but about what you are.
Saint Gregory the Great

*G*ive of your super-abundance to children. Fill your hearts with the love of God, and then you will always be able to instill it into them. If we are united to God, we shall be able to do wonders for them.

Saint Madeleine Sophie Barat

May 23

May 24

*W*hen you encounter
difficulties and contradictions, do not try
to break them, but bend them with gentleness and time.

Saint Francis de Sales

When I look at the condition of my human weakness, my strength is shattered, but when I raise my eyes to the grace of divine assistance I am confident that I can accomplish virtuous deeds.

Saint Bede the Venerable

May 25

May 26

*C*ast yourself confi-
dently into the arms of God. And be very
sure that if God wants anything of you,
he will fit you for the work and give you
the strength to do it.

Saint Philip Neri

$\mathcal{C}$ome, Holy Spirit. Let the precious pearl of the Father and the Word's delight come. Spirit of truth, you are the reward of the saints, the comforter of souls, light in the darkness, riches to the poor, treasure to lovers, food for the hungry, comfort to those who are wandering; to sum up, you are the one in whom all treasures are contained.

Saint Mary Magdalene de Pazzi

May 27

May 28

*F*or the Christian
there is no such thing as a "stranger."
There is only the neighbor—the person
who happens to be next to us, the person
most in need of our help. Whether he is
related to us or not, whether we "like"
him or not, doesn't make any difference.

Saint Teresa Benedicta of the Cross (Edith Stein)

$\mathcal{N}$othing halfhearted for me—I will follow Christ with all my heart and soul.

Saint Thérèse of Lisieux

May 29

*T*he divine heart is an abyss of all blessings, and into it the poor should submerge all their needs. It is an abyss of joy in which all of us can immerse our sorrows. It is an abyss of lowliness to counteract our foolishness, an abyss of mercy for the wretched, an abyss of love to meet our every need.

Saint Margaret Mary Alacoque

*L*et Mary's soul be in each of us to proclaim the greatness of the Lord. Let her spirit be in each to rejoice in the Lord. Christ has only one mother in the flesh, but we all bring forth Christ in faith.

Saint Ambrose

May 31

June

*I*n serenity look forward to the joy that follows sadness.... The well-prepared mind forgets the suffering inflicted from without and glides eagerly to what it has contemplated within.

Saint Peter Damian

June 1

June 2

*C*onsult not your fears
but your hopes and your dreams. Think
not about your frustrations, but about
your unfulfilled potential. Concern yourself
not with what you tried and failed in, but
with what it is still possible for you to do.

Blessed John XXIII

$\mathcal{M}$any seek to love God by different methods, but there is none so short and so easy as to do every-thing for his love.

Saint Elizabeth Ann Seton

June 3

June 4

*T*here is something in
humility which strangely exalts the heart.
Saint Augustine of Hippo

$\mathcal{I}$n her voyage across
the ocean of this world, the Church is like
a great ship being pounded by the waves
of life's different stresses. Our duty is not
to abandon ship but to keep her on
course.

Saint Boniface

June 5

June 6

*I*t shows weakness of
mind to hold too much to the beaten
track through fear of innovations. Times
change, and to keep up with them, we
must modify our methods.

Saint Madeleine Sophie Barat

*W*hat brings joy to the heart is not so much the friend's gift as the friend's love.

Saint Aelred

June 7

June 8

$\mathcal{I}$n the twilight of life, God will not judge us on our earthly possessions and human successes, but on how well we have loved.

Saint John of the Cross

*S*unrise marks the hour for men and women to begin their toil, but in our souls, Lord, prepare a dwelling for the day that will never end.

Saint Ephrem

June 9

June 10

*W*hen did it ever happen that a person had confidence in God and was lost?

Saint Alphonsus Liguori

*W*hat will you do, powerless as you are, to follow God and imitate his perfection? For myself, when I see myself in this powerlessness, I try to lose myself in him. I do my best to forget myself in order to see only him, and, if possible, I speak with him intimately.

Blessed Marie of the Incarnation

June 11

*H*ere is a rule for
everyday life: Do not do anything which
you cannot offer to God.

Saint John Mary Vianney

$\mathcal{I}$f things created are so
full of loveliness, how resplendent with
beauty must be the One who made them!
Saint Anthony of Padua

June 13

June 14

Nothing richer can be offered to God than a good will, for good will is the originator of all good and the mother of all virtues. Whoever begins to have that good will has secured all the help needed for living well.

Saint Albert the Great

$\mathcal{B}$e careful, above all, of charity toward God, your neighbor, and yourself. Refrain from judging any-one whomsoever, except when it is your duty to do so.

Saint Pio of Pietrelcina

June 15

June 16

*G*od wills that here in
this life we always remain at his table of
graces, since he wants to have us at the
table of his glory for all eternity.

Saint Vincent Pallotti

*G*entleness is not weakness when it draws its source from the heart of Jesus and flows like honey from the mouth of the lion. This is what we must bring into our way of governing, moderate structures and words of gentleness. But we must insist that people continue to grow.

Saint Madeleine Sophie Barat

June 17

June 18

*O*h, how good and
pleasant a thing it is to dwell in the heart
of Jesus! Who is there that does not love
a heart so wounded? Who can refuse a
return of love to a heart so loving?

Saint Bernard of Clairvaux

$\mathcal{J}$ resolved always to prefer labors to comforts, contempt to honors. And, in particular, if on one side a kingdom were offered and on the other the washing of dishes, I would refuse the kingdom and accept the dishwashing so as to be truly like Christ, who humbled himself.

Saint John Berchmans

June 19

June 20

$\mathcal{I}$t is such a folly to pass one's time fretting, instead of resting quietly on the heart of Jesus.

Saint Thérèse of Lisieux

*W*e should never
desire to be over others. Instead, we
ought to be servants who are submissive
to every human being for God's sake.

Saint Francis of Assisi

June 21

June 22

$\mathcal{I}$ will not mistrust [God]...though I feel myself weakening and on the verge of being overcome with fear. I shall remember how Saint Peter, at a blast of wind, began to sink..., and I shall do as he did: call upon Christ and pray to him for help. And then I trust he shall place his holy hand on me and in the stormy seas hold me up from drowning.

Saint Thomas More

*H*eaven is filled with converted sinners of all kinds, and there is room for more.

Saint Joseph Cafasso

June 23

June 24

One who governs one's
passions is master of the world. We must
either rule them or be ruled by them. It is
better to be the hammer than the anvil.

Saint Dominic

$\mathcal{I}$f you want God to hear your prayers, hear the voice of the poor. If you wish God to anticipate your wants, provide those of the needy without waiting for them to ask you.

Saint Thomas of Villanova

June 25

June 26

*S*eek the highest wisdom not by arguments in words, but by the perfection of your life, not by speech, but by the faith that comes from simplicity of heart....

Saint Columban

*W*orry over our health
will not improve our health.

Saint Teresa of Avila

June 27

*I*f we are not to be scorched and made unfruitful, we need the dew of God.... Through the Spirit, the image and inscription of the Father and the Son have been given to us, and it is our duty to use the coin committed to our charge and make it yield a rich profit for the Lord.

Saint Irenaeus

*H*oliness is virtue at high tension; it is the impetus and poetry of goodness.... Saints are not worn-out, half-awake people who cannot make up their minds to do their share in life. For Saint Paul, holiness is the fullness of human maturity.... Holiness is life, movement, nobility, and effervescence.

Blessed James Alberione

June 29

*L*ove is sufficient of itself, it gives pleasure by itself and because of itself. It is its own merit, its own reward. Love looks for no cause outside itself, no effect beyond itself. Its profit lies in its practice.

Saint Bernard of Clairvaux

July

*L*et us try not to be exacting with others, but rather pass over in silence those thousand little annoyances that tend to embitter us. We know that no one is perfect in this life, and we must put up with the defects of others.

Saint Rose Philippine Duchesne

July 1

July 2

*O*ne must see God
in everyone.

Saint Catherine Labouré

*T*he best way to pre-
pare for death is to spend every day of
life as though it were the last. Think of
the end of worldly honor, wealth, and
pleasure and ask yourself: And then?
And then?

Saint Philip Neri

July 3

$\mathcal{T}$o be simple is to be like a sunflower which follows all the movements of the sun and ever turns toward it.

Saint Julie Billiart

*T*he one who exalts us even before the world is God, and God alone. Every honor that comes to us should reflect God, or we must despise it. Does the Lord permit a small humiliation? So be it. Oh, if we only knew the great value of these humiliations!

Blessed John XXIII

July 5

July 6

$\mathcal{B}$lessed is the servant
who safeguards the secrets of the Lord in
her heart.

Saint Francis of Assisi

*O*f what use are revelations, visions, feelings of God's presence, sweetnesses from him? Of what use are gifts of wisdom, elevations? Of what use even is contemplation? Indeed, all these are useless unless one has true knowledge of God and of self.

Blessed Angela of Foligno

July 7

July 8

*L*earning unsupported
by grace may get into our ears; it never
reaches the heart.

Saint Isidore

*L*et's work for heaven:
all the rest is nothing.

Saint Bernadette Soubirous

July 9

*T*here can be no per-
fect virtue, none that bears fruit, unless it
be exercised by means of our neighbor.

Saint Catherine of Siena

*J*esus, I feel within me a great desire to please you, but, at the same time, I feel totally incapable of doing this without your special light and help, which I can expect only from you. Accomplish your will within me—even in spite of me.

Saint Claude de la Colombière

July 11

July 12

*D*o you hate to be
deceived? Then never deceive another.

Saint John Chrysostom

Our Lord has created persons for all states in life, and in all of them we see people who have achieved sanctity by fulfilling their obligations well.... The different states of life are like so many roads that lead to the Lord.

Saint Anthony Mary Claret

July 13

July 14

$\mathcal{I}$f Christ Jesus dwells in us as friend and noble leader, we can endure all things, for Christ helps and strengthens us and never abandons us.

Saint Teresa of Avila

When hen we pray, the
voice of the heart must be heard more
than the proceedings from the mouth.

Saint Bonaventure

July 15

I will say of the cross what an Eastern proverb says of patience: it is a tree with bitter roots, but sweet flowers and fruit. Find sweetness in doing everything in the will of the Lord.

Blessed John XXIII

$\mathcal{M}$ake many acts of love, for they set the soul on fire and make it gentle. Whatever you do, offer it up to God, and pray it may be for his honor and glory.

Saint Teresa of Avila

July 17

July 18

*I*f there were no poor
people in the world, it would be necessary to dig to the center of the earth to
look for them and rescue them, to show
them compassion and do them good.

Saint Camillus de Lellis

*W*hat do you wish for, what do you pray for, my dear brothers and sisters, when you come to church? Is it mercy? How can it be anything else? Show mercy, then, while you are on earth, and mercy will be shown to you in heaven.

Saint Caesarius of Arles

July 19

*D*o not fear what may happen tomorrow. The same loving Father who cares for you today will care for you tomorrow and every day. Either he will shield you from suffering or he will give you the unfailing strength to bear it. Be at peace, then, and put aside all anxious thoughts and imaginings.

Saint Francis de Sales

$\mathcal{D}$o not believe only
what the eyes of your body tell you.
What is not seen is here more truly seen,
for what is seen belongs to time, but
what is not seen belongs to eternity.

Saint Ambrose

July 21

July 22

*W*hen we cast our
faults into the devouring fire of Love with
total, childlike trust, how would they not
be consumed, so that nothing is left of
them?

Saint Thérèse of Lisieux

*R*emember, O Lord, my poverty; forgive me my sins. In the place where iniquity abounds, let your grace abound. Take not away from your people the grace of the Holy Spirit.

Saint Gregory of Nazianzen

July 23

*H*ope everything from the mercy of God. It is as boundless as his power.

Saint Frances of Rome

γou do well to desire to
be united with God every day, and the
best proof of this is that whenever you
can, you never neglect to go to Jesus in
the Blessed Sacrament to give and receive
the kiss of peace.

Saint Pio of Pietrelcina

July 25

*G*od bids us to be
peace-loving, harmonious, and of one
mind in his house.... The greatest offering we can make to God is our peace....

Saint Cyprian

*L*ord Jesus, take me
away from myself, and take my place;
may my life be destroyed, and your life
be my life.

Saint Vincent Pallotti

July 27

July 28

$\mathcal{W}$e have to let Jesus know our pain, our fears, our hopes, our remorse, and our doubts.... He will cure everything. He will enlighten our mind, strengthen our will, and fill our hearts with joy.

Blessed James Alberione

*A*ll shall be well, and all shall be well, and all manner of things shall be well.

Blessed Julian of Norwich

July 29

July 30

*J*f you hope for mercy, show mercy.
If you look for kindness,
   show kindness.
If you want to receive, give.
If you ask for yourself what you
   deny to others, your asking is a
   mockery.

Saint Peter Chrysologus

$\mathcal{J}$f he who was without sin prayed, how much more ought sinners to pray?

Saint Cyprian

July 31

August

$\mathcal{A}$ll the merit of
virtue lies in the will. Sometimes one who
wishes to believe has more merit than
another who does believe.

Saint Alphonsus Liguori

August 1

*W*e are too little to
be able always to rise above difficulties.
Well, then, let us pass beneath them
quite simply.

Saint Thérèse of Lisieux

We were born to love, we live to love, and we will die to love still more.

Saint Joseph Cafasso

August 3

August 4

*L*ife is given us that we may learn to die well, and we never think of it! To die well we must live well.

Saint John Mary Vianney

$\mathcal{S}$ince the salvation of humanity began through the Hail Mary, the salvation of each individual is linked with this prayer.... This same prayer, devoutly said, will cause the word of God to germinate in our souls, and to bear the fruit of life: Jesus Christ.

Saint Louis de Montfort

August 5

August 6

There are moments when I mistrust myself, when I feel my own weakness and wretchedness in the most profound depths of my own being, and I have noticed that I can endure such moments only by trusting in the infinite mercy of God. Patience, prayer, and silence—these are what give strength to the soul.

Saint Faustina Kowalska

*T*his is my happiness, this my pleasure: to live with Jesus, to walk with Jesus, to converse with Jesus—to suffer with and for him, this is my treasure.

Saint Alphonsus Rodriguez

August 7

August 8

*A*rm yourself with
prayer rather than a sword; wear humility
rather than fine clothes.

Saint Dominic

$\mathcal{M}$y desire for truth
was itself a prayer.
Saint Teresa Benedicta of the Cross (Edith Stein)

August 9

August 10

*P*rudence must precede every action that we undertake, for, if prudence be wanting, there is nothing, however good it may seem, which is not turned into evil.

Saint Basil the Great

*G*aze upon Christ.
Consider him. Contemplate him and
desire to imitate him.

Saint Clare of Assisi

August 11

August 12

$\mathcal{I}$ have never had doubts about the faith. But something has left me dismayed. For 2,000 years Christ has remained on the cross with his arms outstretched. Where are we with the proclamation of the Good News?

Blessed John XXIII

*E*arth has no sorrow
that heaven cannot heal.

Saint Thomas More

August 13

August 14

*H*ere below we can
only work with one hand, because we
need the other hand to hold fast to the
Immaculata so that we don't fall. In heaven we will have both hands free, and the
Mother of God will be our guardian.

Saint Maximilian Kolbe

*A*ll the way to heaven is heaven, because Jesus is the way.
Saint Catherine of Siena

August 15

August 16

*G*od does not insist or desire that we should mourn in agony of heart; rather, it is his wish that out of love for him we should rejoice with laughter in our soul.

Saint John Climacus

*T*ry to enter the treasure chamber that is within you, and then you discover the treasure chamber of heaven. They are one and the same. If you succeed in entering one, you will see both.

Saint Isaac of Syria

August 17

August 18

*T*he martyrdom of love cannot be relegated to a second place, for love is as strong as death. For the martyrs of love suffer infinitely more in remaining in this life so as to serve God than if they died a thousand times over in testimony to their faith and love and fidelity.

Saint Jane Frances de Chantal

*T*he Christian life is the continuation and completion of the life of Christ in us. We should be so many Christs here on earth, continuing his life and his words, laboring and suffering in a holy and divine manner in the Spirit of Jesus.

Saint John Eudes

August 19

*L*earn the lesson that if
you are to do the work of a prophet, what
you need is not a scepter but a hoe.

Saint Bernard of Clairvaux

*H*ope has been the sole companion of my life, the greatest aid in doubts, the strongest assistance in my weakness; not hope in men—which is thought to bring greater happiness and instead brings greater disaster—but hope in Christ, supported by the heavenly promise that he will strengthen the weakest of men with a greatness of soul and divine help.

Saint Pius X

August 21

August 22

*T*hough she was the
Mother of the Lord, yet Mary desired to
learn the precepts of the Lord, and she
who brought forth God, yet desired to
know God.

Saint Ambrose

*A*part from the cross, there is no other ladder by which we may get to heaven.

Saint Rose of Lima

August 23

August 24

O Jesus, you are my
true friend, my only friend. You take a
part in all my misfortunes; you take them
upon yourself, you know how to change
them into blessings.

Saint Claude de la Colombiére

$\mathcal{E}$verything begins with prayer, spending a little time on our knees.... If all the world's rulers and leaders would spend a little time on their knees before God, I believe we would have a better world.

Blessed Teresa of Calcutta

August 25

August 26

*T*he most Blessed
Sacrament is Christ made visible. The poor
sick person is Christ again made visible.

Saint Gerard Majella

*S*anctify yourself and
you will sanctify society.

Saint Francis of Assisi

August 27

*T*oo late have I loved you, O Beauty so ancient and so new, too late have I loved you! You were with me, but I was not with you. You cried out and pierced my deafness. You enlightened my blindness. I tasted you and I am hungry for you. You touched me, and I am afire with longing for your embrace.

Saint Augustine of Hippo

One must always be ready, for death comes when and where God wills it.

Saint John Neumann

August 29

August 30

*A*ctions speak louder
than words; let your words teach and
your actions speak.

Saint Anthony of Padua

*T*he faith given me in baptism suggests to me surely: of yourself you will do nothing, but if you have God as the center of all your actions, you will reach the goal.

Blessed Pier Giorgio Frassati

August 31

September

*T*o reach something
good it is very useful to have gone astray,
and thus to have acquired experience.

Saint Teresa of Avila

September 1

September 2

*J*esus Christ, in his infinite wisdom, used the words and idioms
that were in use among those whom he
addressed. You should do likewise.

Saint Joseph Cafasso

*T*he sacrament of Reconciliation is the great means of perfection. Confession is the channel of special sanctifying grace; it is the restoration of lost energies, light for the new journey, movement of our heart toward resolution, blessing and divine approval of our daily journey toward God.

Blessed James Alberione

September 3

September 4

It is better to make penitents by gentleness than hypocrites by severity.

Saint Francis de Sales

*J*esus is the Life I want
to live, the Light I want to reflect, the
Way to the Father, the Love I want to
express, the Joy I want to share, the
Peace I want to sow around me. Jesus is
everything to me.

Blessed Teresa of Calcutta

September 5

September 6

*N*ot everyone can become a genius, but the path of holiness is open to all.

Saint Maximilian Kolbe

A glad spirit attains
to perfection more quickly than any other.
Saint Philip Neri

September 7

*T*he quintessence of love is sacrifice and suffering. Truth wears a crown of thorns. Prayer involves the intellect, the will, and the emotions.

Saint Faustina Kowalska

$\mathcal{L}$earn to defend your convictions without hating your adversaries, and love those who think differently from yourselves.

Blessed Frederic Ozanam

September 9

September 10

*W*hen night comes,
and you look back over the day and see
how fragmentary everything has been,
and how much you planned that has
gone undone, and all the reasons you
have to be embarrassed and ashamed,
just take everything exactly as it is, put
it in God's hands, and leave it with him.
Then you will be able to rest in him—
really rest—and start the next day as a
new life.

Saint Teresa Benedicta of the Cross (Edith Stein)

$\mathcal{M}$any people have difficulty finding a meditation book. But I have found nothing so good as my own heart and the heart of Jesus. Why is it that we so often change the subject of our meditation? Only one thing is necessary: Jesus Christ. Think unceasingly of him.

Saint John Gabriel Perboyre

September 11

September 12

*I*t is better to remain
silent and to be than to talk and not be.

Saint Ignatius of Antioch

$\mathcal{I}$t gives more praise to God and more delight if we pray, steadfast in love, trusting in his goodness, clinging to him by grace, than if we ask for everything our thoughts can name.

Blessed Julian of Norwich

September 13

September 14

*W*hen you become
true lovers of the Crucified, you will
always celebrate the feast of the cross in
the inner temple of the soul, bearing all in
silence and not relying on any creature.

Saint Paul of the Cross

*T*he acceptable offering of spiritual purification is accomplished not in a man-made temple, but in the recesses of the heart where the Lord Jesus freely enters.

Saint Lawrence Justinian

September 15

September 16

*Y*ou cannot have God for
your Father if you have not the Church
for your mother.

Saint Cyprian

*T*he school of Christ is
the school of charity. On the last day,
when the great general examination
takes place, there will be no question
at all on the text of Aristotle, the apho-
risms of Hippocrates, or the paragraphs
of Justinian. Charity will be the whole
syllabus.

Saint Robert Bellarmine

September 17

September 18

*H*owever just your words, you spoil everything when you speak with anger.

Saint John Chrysostom

$\mathcal{Y}$ou can be certain of
this: if you practice love within your own
family, God will help you outside it.

Saint Alphonsus Liguori

September 19

September 20

*I*n loving your neighbor...you are on a journey. Where are you traveling if not to the Lord God? We have not yet reached God's presence, but we have our neighbor at our side. Support, then, this companion of your pilgrimage if you want to come into the presence of the One with whom you desire to remain forever.

Saint Augustine of Hippo

*W*e have no knowl-
edge of our way unless we follow Jesus,
always working, always suffering.

Saint Louise de Marillac

September 21

September 22

*T*he heart of a Christian, who believes and feels, cannot pass by the hardships and deprivations of the poor without helping them.

Blessed Louis Guanella

$\mathcal{I}$ know from my own experience that the best way to avoid falling is to lean on the cross of Jesus with confidence in him alone who, for our salvation, desired to be nailed to it.

Saint Pio of Pietrelcina

September 23

September 24

*A*bove all preserve peace of heart. This is more valuable than any treasure. In order to preserve it there is nothing more useful than renouncing your own will and substituting for it the will of the divine heart.

Saint Margaret Mary Alacoque

$\mathcal{F}$or us the fear of God consists wholly in love, and perfect love of God brings our fear of him to its perfection. Our love for God is entrusted with its own responsibility: to observe his counsels, to obey his laws, to trust his promises.

Saint Hilary

September 25

September **26**

$\mathcal{I}$f you speak of God,
speak with love. If you speak of yourself,
speak with love. Take care that there is
nothing in you but love, love, love.

Saint Bernardine of Siena

*E*xtend mercy toward others, so that there can be no one in need whom you met without helping. Just consider how much we ourselves are in need of mercy. For what hope is there for us if God should withdraw mercy from us?

Saint Vincent de Paul

September 27

September 28

*B*y your work you
show what you love and what you know.
Saint Bruno

*R*epentance is the
renewal of one's Baptism.

Saint John Climacus

September 29

September 30

*I*gnorance of the
Scriptures is ignorance of Christ.

Saint Jerome

October

$\mathcal{I}$n the heart of the
Church, my mother, I will be love, and
thus I will be all things, as my desire
finds its direction.

St. Thérèse of Lisieux

October 1

*M*ake yourself
familiar with the angels, and behold them
frequently in spirit; for, without being
seen, they are present with you.

Saint Francis de Sales

$\mathcal{I}$t is a great thing, this reading of the Scriptures! For it is not possible ever to exhaust the mind of the Scriptures. It is a well that has no bottom.

Saint John Chrysostom

October 3

October 4

*P*reach the Gospel
always. If necessary, use words.

Saint Francis of Assisi

$\mathcal{I}$ do not understand how it is possible not to trust in him who can do all things. With him, everything; without him, nothing. He is Lord. He will not allow those who have placed all their trust in him to be put to shame.

Saint Faustina Kowalska

October 5

*S*mall children give small gifts; but God divinizes his children, bestowing on them qualities conformable to their high dignity.

Blessed Marie of the Incarnation

*T*he Rosary is the
most complete and easiest instruction
about the Blessed Mother, and it is the
source of devotion to the Divine Master.
Blessed Timothy Giaccardo

October 7

*G*o and find Jesus when your patience and strength give out and you feel alone and helpless.... Say to him: "Jesus, you know exactly what is going on. You are all I have, and you know all. Come to my help." And then go and don't worry about how you are going to manage. That you have told God about it is enough. He has a good memory.

Blessed Jeanne Jugan

*W*henever I see so
many poor brothers and neighbors of
mine suffering beyond their strength and
overwhelmed with so many physical or
mental ills that I cannot alleviate, then I
become exceedingly sorrowful; but I trust
in Christ, who knows my heart.

Saint John of God

October 9

$\mathcal{M}$y hope is in God, who has only us with whom to fulfill his plans. It is for us to be faithful and not to spoil his work by our cowardice.

Saint Isaac Jogues

γou can love this life all you want, as long as you know what to choose.

Saint Augustine of Hippo

October 11

October 12

*T*ime is like loose
change. It is given to us here below to
buy the real things of eternity.

Saint Julie Billiart

$\mathcal{A}$ friend is long
sought, hardly found, and with difficulty
kept.

Saint Jerome

October 13

October 14

*L*ove totally him who
gave himself totally for your love.

Saint Clare of Assisi

*L*et nothing disturb you.
Let nothing frighten you.
All things are passing.
God alone does not change.
Patience achieves everything.
Whoever has God lacks nothing.
God alone suffices.

Saint Teresa of Avila

October 15

October **16**

*T*he Sacred Heart is an inexhaustible fountain, and its sole desire is to pour itself out into the hearts of the humble so as to free them and prepare them to lead lives according to his good pleasure.

Saint Margaret Mary Alacoque

*I*n your harmony together of mind and heart, the song you sing is Jesus Christ. Every one of you should form a choir, so that, in harmony of sound through harmony of hearts, and in unity taking the note from God, you may sing with one voice through Jesus Christ to the Father.

Saint Ignatius of Antioch

October 17

October 18

*G*o to Holy Communion
even when you feel lukewarm, leaving
everything in God's hands. The more my
sickness debilitates me, the more urgent-
ly do I need a doctor.

Saint Bonaventure

$\mathcal{I}$ do not pray for success. I ask for faithfulness.

Blessed Teresa of Calcutta

October 19

*I*f you cannot spend much time at prayer, no matter: to act well is always to pray well. Be attentive to your duties and at the same time be attentive to God by frequently purifying your heart in the immense ocean of divine love.

Saint Paul of the Cross

$\mathscr{B}$e merry, really merry. The life of a true Christian should be a perpetual jubilee, a prelude to the festivals of eternity.

Blessed Théophane Vénard

October 21

October 22

O Mary, you lead me to
know Jesus Christ, the Divine Master, you
give him to me, you bring me to him, and
with boundless love you unite me in one-
ness of life with this Master who lives in
the Church.

Blessed Timothy Giaccardo

*W*ell-ordered self-love
is right and natural.

Saint Thomas Aquinas

October 23

October 24

*A*pproach Jesus according to the event you are meditating on. Imagine that you are standing alongside him. Picture him wearing the same clothing he wore when he walked through this world.... Imagine that Jesus Christ is saying to you, "Come, pray with me. Could you not watch and pray one hour with me?"

Saint Anthony Mary Claret

*W*e are the grain of
wheat dying in the earth; can we repine
at such a destiny? But we are full of confidence and wholly animated with
courage to persevere, hoping that some-
day our work will bear fruit. It matters
little whether we taste of it in this life,
provided only that we serve God's cause.

Saint Rose Philippine Duchesne

October 25

October 26

*W*e shall steer safely through every storm, so long as our heart is right, our intention fervent, our courage steadfast, and our trust fixed on God. If at times we are somewhat stunned by the tempest, never fear. Let us take a breath, and go on afresh.

Saint Francis de Sales

γou will effect more by kind words and by a courteous manner than by anger or sharp rebuke, which should never be used except in necessity.

Saint Angela Merici

October 27

October 28

We need to fall and
we need to see that we have done so. For
if we never fell we should not know how
weak and pitiable we are in ourselves.
Nor should we fully know the wonderful
love of our Maker.

Blessed Julian of Norwich

*H*oly Communion is
the shortest and safest way to heaven.

Saint Pius X

October *29*

October 30

*T*he important thing is
not to think much, but to love much; and
so do that which best stirs you to love.

Saint Teresa of Avila

*O*h, how good is the
good God!

Saint Julie Billiart

October 31

November

*W*hat saint has ever won the crown without first contending for it?

Saint Jerome

November 1

$\mathcal{L}$et us be like the swan. When it is dying it gathers all its inner forces and sings with more harmony than ever before in its life. That is how saints die. It is the purest act of their life, the one most burning with love, the most perfect.

Saint Madeleine Sophie Barat

$\mathcal{N}$othing should
upset a servant of God except sin.

Saint Francis of Assisi

$\mathcal{N}$ovember 3

November 4

$\mathcal{I}$n meditation we find
the strength to bring Christ to birth in
ourselves and in others.

Saint Charles Borromeo

$\mathcal{E}$njoy yourself as much
as you like—if only you keep from sin.
Saint John Bosco

November 5

$\mathcal{N}$ovember 6

$\mathcal{W}$e may be excused
for not always being bright, but we are
not excused for not being always gra-
cious, yielding, and considerate.

Saint Francis de Sales

γou come across num-
bers of unfortunate people whom you are
not able to comfort. God also sees them.
Has God not the power to give them
greater comfort and assistance? Carry
their cross and burden for them. Do your
utmost to give them some little relief—
that is in your power—and remain at
peace.

Saint Louise de Marillac

November 7

November 8

*L*et us live for love,
always surrendered, immolating ourselves at every moment, by doing God's
will without searching for extraordinary
things. Then let us make ourselves quite
tiny, allowing ourselves to be carried, like
a babe in its mother's arms, by him who
is our All....

Blessed Elizabeth of the Trinity

*I*f we wish to enter
again into the enjoyment of Truth as into
paradise, we must enter through faith in,
hope in, and love of Jesus Christ, the
Mediator between God and humanity,
who is like the tree of life in the middle
of paradise.

Saint Bonaventure

November 9

*R*emember, Christian, the surpassing worth of the wisdom that is yours. Bear in mind the kind of school in which you are to learn your skills, the rewards to which you are called. Mercy itself wishes you to be merciful. Righteousness itself wishes you to be righteous, so that the Creator may shine forth in the creature, and the image of God be reflected in the mirror of the human heart....

Saint Leo the Great

*T*o pass judgment on another is to usurp shamelessly a prerogative of God, and to condemn is to ruin one's soul.

Saint John Climacus

*N*ovember *11*

November 12

*U*nion with God is a
song which does not die in the hearing,
a flavor which does not abate in the eat-
ing, an embrace which gives delight
without end.

Saint Augustine of Hippo

*L*ord, you are the one who acts. I am not even an instrument in your hands, as others say. You alone are the one who does all, and I am nothing more than a spectator of the great and wonderful works that you know how to accomplish.

Saint Frances Xavier Cabrini

November 13

November 14

I find a heaven in the
midst of saucepans and brooms.

Saint Stanislaus Kostka

*G*od did not tell us to follow him because he needed our help, but because he knew that loving him would make us whole.

Saint Irenaeus

November 15

*M*ay my soul bless you, O Lord God my Creator, may my soul bless you. From the very core of my being may all your merciful gifts sing your praise. Your generous care for your daughter has been rich in mercy; indeed it has been immeasurable, and as far as I am able I give you thanks.

Saint Gertrude

*E*verything we gain
comes from what we give.

Saint Teresa of Avila

November 17

November 18

*S*ince, by the goodness of God, we who are called "Christians" have been granted the honor of sharing this name—the greatest, the highest, the most sublime of all names—it follows that each of the titles that express its meaning should be clearly reflected in us. If we are not to lie when we call ourselves "Christians," we must bear witness to it by our way of living.

                                        Saint Gregory of Nyssa

*W*hat words can adequately describe God's gifts? They are so numerous that they defy enumeration. They are so great that any one of them demands our total gratitude in response.

Saint Basil the Great

November 19

November 20

*M*ay you be sub-
merged, invaded by the great river of
Love. May you feel the springs of living
water well up from the deepest part of
your soul, so that God may be your all.

Blessed Elizabeth of the Trinity

$\mathcal{I}$f you are wise, then know that you have been created for the glory of God and your own eternal salvation. This is your goal; this is the center of your life; this is the treasure of your heart.

Saint Robert Bellarmine

November 21

November 22

*A*t each step one marvels at the grandeur, the power, and goodness of our God. How generously he has provided for our wants—I would almost say, for our pleasures.

Blessed Mother Theodore Guerin

*W*ho can express the binding power of divine love? Who can find words for the splendor of its beauty? Beyond all description are the heights to which love lifts us. Love unites us to God. It cancels innumerable sins, has no limits to its endurance, and bears everything patiently. Love is neither servile nor arrogant.... By it, all God's chosen ones have been sanctified; without it, it is impossible to please him.

Saint Clement I

November 23

November 24

*T*he greater and more persistent your confidence in God, the more abundantly you will receive all that you ask.

Saint Albert the Great

*W*hen I go into the chapel, I place myself before the good God and I say to him: "Lord, here I am, give me what you like." If he gives me something, I am well pleased and I thank him. If he gives me nothing, again I thank him, because that is all I deserve. And then, I tell him everything that comes into my mind; I tell him my troubles and my joys, and I listen.

Saint Catherine Labouré

November 25

November 26

*H*oliness is, and
always consists in, living Jesus Christ as
he is presented in the Gospel: the Way,
the Truth, and the Life.

Blessed James Alberione

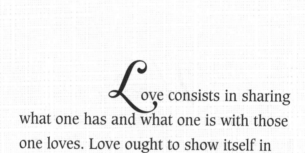

*L*ove consists in sharing what one has and what one is with those one loves. Love ought to show itself in deeds more than in words.

Saint Ignatius of Loyola

November 27

November 28

*I*n all created things dis-
cern the providence and wisdom of God,
and in all things give him thanks.

Saint Teresa of Avila

*P*rayer...gives joy to the spirit, peace to the heart. I speak of prayer, not words. It is the longing for God, love too deep for words.

Saint John Chrysostom

November 29

November 30

*A*dversity shows
what the spirit of a person is made of.
Saint Alphonsus Liguori

December

*T*he best prayer is to
rest in the goodness of God.

Blessed Julian of Norwich

December 1

December 2

*A*nd so, children of justice, follow John's exhortation: Make straight the way of the Lord. Remove all obstacles and stumbling blocks so that you will be able to go straight along the road to eternal life. Through a sincere faith prepare yourselves so that you may be free to receive the Holy Spirit.

Saint Cyril of Jerusalem

*I*t is a glorious privilege
that God should grant us his eternal
image.... We must turn back our image
undefiled and holy to our God and Father,
for he is holy.... We must restore his
image with love, for he is love.... We
must restore it with loyalty and truth, for
he is loyal and truthful.

Saint Columban

December 3

December 4

*L*ead me to pastures, Lord, and graze there with me. Do not let my heart lean either to the right or to the left, but let your good Spirit guide me along the straight path. Whatever I do, let it be in accordance with your will, now until the end.

Saint John Damascene

*S*imply by making us wait, God increases our desire, which in turn enlarges the capacity of our soul, making it able to receive what is to be given us. So...let us continue to desire, for we shall be filled.

Saint Augustine of Hippo

December 5

*J*esus likes to intervene in the smallest details of our life, and he often fulfills secret wishes of mine that I sometimes hide from him, although I know that from him nothing can be hidden.

Saint Faustina Kowalska

*I*n Christ we are all things; he is everything to us. If you have wounds to heal, he is a physician; if fever scorches you, he is a fountain.... If you need help, he is strength; if you fear death, he is life; if you hunger, he is food.

Saint Ambrose

December 7

*T*o whom should we turn for help in practicing virtue and charity if not to Mary? She is all charity. Wherever Mary is, there is charity.... In the Christian world, the Head is Jesus Christ and the Heart is the Virgin Mary.

Saint Anthony Mary Claret

*P*rivate prayer is like straw scattered here and there; if you set it on fire it makes a lot of little flames. But gather these straws into a bundle and light them, and you get a mighty fire, rising like a column into the sky; public prayer is like that.

Saint John Mary Vianney

December 9

December 10

Never lie down to sleep without having first examined your conscience on the way you have spent the day and without first turning your thoughts to God.

Saint Pio of Pietrelcina

*S*eek God in all things
and we shall find God by our side.

Saint Peter Claver

December 11

December 12

*Y*ield yourself fully to God and you will find out [what martyrdom of love is like]! Divine love takes its sword to the hidden recesses of our inmost soul and divides us from ourselves.

Saint Jane Frances de Chantal

*Y*ou are children of eternity. Your immortal crown awaits you, and the best of fathers waits there to reward your duty and love. You may indeed sow here in tears, but you may be sure there to reap in joy.

Saint Elizabeth Ann Seton

December 13

December 14

*W*here there is no love,
pour love in, and you will pull
love out.

Saint John of the Cross

*C*hrist made love the stairway that would enable all Christians to climb to heaven. Hold fast to it, therefore, in all sincerity. Give one another practical proof of it, and by your progress in it, make your ascent together.

Saint Fulgentius of Ruspe

December 15

December 16

It is confidence and nothing else that leads one to love. And what offends Jesus, what wounds his heart, is lack of trust in him.

Saint Thérèse of Lisieux

$\mathcal{I}$f I look at myself I am nothing. But if I look at us all I am hopeful; for I see the unity of love among all my fellow Christians. In this unity lies our salvation.

Blessed Julian of Norwich

December 17

December 18

*F*ight all error, but
do it with good humor, patience, kindness, and love. Harshness will damage
your own soul and spoil the best cause.

Saint John of Kanty

$\mathscr{A}$ servant of God
ought always to be happy.

Saint Philip Neri

December 19

December 20

*A*s those who see
light are in the light sharing its brilliance,
so those who see God are in God sharing
his glory, and that glory gives them life.
To see God is to share in life.

Saint Irenaeus

*J*esus is honey in the mouth, music in the ear, and a shout of joy in the heart.

Saint Bernard of Clairvaux

December 21

December 22

*I*n a way, every
Christian is to be a bride of God's Word, a
mother of Christ, his daughter and sister,
at once virginal and fruitful. These words
are used in a universal sense for the
Church, in a special sense for Mary, in a
particular sense for the individual
Christian. They are used by God's Wisdom
in person, the Word of the Father.

Blessed Isaac of Stella

*G*od desires that graces must come to us from the hands of Christ, through his most sacred humanity, in which God takes delight.

Saint Teresa of Avila

December 23

December 24

*I*t was indeed wondrous
that Christ was conceived in a womb, but
it is no less striking that he be borne in
our hearts.

Saint Peter Damian

*T*his, Lord, is your
Word to us, this is your all-powerful message: while all things were in midnight
silence..., he came from his royal throne,
...the gentle apostle of love.

Blessed William of St.-Thierry

December 25

December 26

*G*od himself is the
reward and end of all our labors.

Saint Thomas Aquinas

*T*he Word of God, born once in the flesh (such is his kindness and his goodness), is always willing to be born spiritually in those who desire him.

Saint Maximus

December 27

*W*hatever happens,
abide steadfast in a determination to
cling simply to God.

Saint Francis de Sales

*R*emember how the crown was attained by those whose sufferings gave new radiance to their faith. The whole company of saints bears witness to the unfailing truth that without real effort no one wins the crown.

Saint Thomas Becket

December 29

December 30

*W*ith God's help and
blessing, we will do all we can to make
our new family a little cenacle where
Jesus will reign over all our affections,
desires, and actions.

Saint Gianna Beretta Molla

*L*et this hope of mine be in my thoughts and on my tongue; let my heart be filled with it, my voice speak of it; let my soul hunger for it, my body thirst for it, my whole being yearn for it until I enter into the joy of the Lord, who is Three in One, blessed for ever. Amen.

Saint Anselm

December 31

Sources

Aelred: *The Office of Readings.*

Albert the Great: *The Office of Readings.*

Alphonsus Liguori: St. Alphonsus Liguori, *The Practice of the Love of Jesus Christ.* Liguori, Missouri: Liguori Publications, 1997; Frederick M. Jones, C.S.S.R., *Alphonsus de Liguori.* Westminster, Maryland: Christian Classics, 1992.

Alphonsus Rodriguez: *Hearts on Fire: Praying with Jesuits.* St. Louis, Missouri: The Institute of Jesuit Sources, 1993.

Ambrose: *The Office of Readings.*

Andrew Kim: Enzo Lodi, *Saints of the Roman Calendar.* Staten Island, New York: Alba House, 1992.

Andrew of Crete: *The Office of Readings.*

Angela Merici: Enzo Lodi, *Saints of the Roman Calendar.* Staten Island, New York: Alba House, 1992; Sr. M. Monica, *Angela Merici and Her Teaching Idea.* New York: Longmans, Green & Co., (c) 1927.

Angela of Foligno: *Angela of Foligno: Complete Works (The Classics of Western Spirituality).* New York: Paulist Press, 1993.

Anselm: *The Office of Readings.*

Anthony Mary Claret: Juan Maria Lozano, C.M.F., *Mystic and Man of Action.* Chicago, Illinois: Claretian Publications, 1977.

Anthony of Padua: Don Mullan, *A Little Book of St. Anthony.* Boston, Massachusetts: Pauline Books & Media, 2003; *The Office of Readings;* SoultoSpirit, www.soultospirit.com/teachers/quotes/wisdom_living/jesus.asp.

Augustine: *Augustine of Hippo: Selected Writings (The Classics of Western Spirituality).* New York: Paulist Press, 1988; *Confessions,* in *Nicene & Post-Nicene Fathers of the Christian Church.* Grand Rapids, Michigan: Wm. B. Eerdmans Publishing Company, 1983; *The Office of Readings.*

Basil the Great: *The Office of Readings.*

Bede: *The Office of Readings.*

Benedict: *The Office of Readings.*

Bernadette Soubirous: René Laurentin, *Bernadette Speaks.* Boston, Massachusetts: Pauline Books & Media, 2000.

Bernard of Clairvaux: *Bernard of Clairvaux: Collected Works (The Classics of Western Spirituality).* New York: Paulist Press, 1987; *The Office of Readings.*

Bernardine of Siena: *The Office of Readings.*

Bonaventure: *Bonaventure: The Soul's Journey into God; The Tree of Life; The Life of St. Francis (The Classics of Western Spirituality).* New York: Paulist Press, 1978.

Boniface: *The Office of Readings.*

Braulio: *The Office of Readings.*

Bruno: *The Office of Readings.*

Caesarius of Arles: *The Office of Readings.*

Camillus de Lellis: Enzo Lodi, *Saints of the Roman Calendar.* Staten Island, New York: Alba House, 1992.

Catherine Labouré: *The Silence of Saint Catherine Labouré.* Fresno, California: Academy Library Guild, 1953.

Catherine of Genoa: *Catherine of Genoa: Purgation and Purgatory; The Spiritual Dialogue (The Classics of Western Spirituality).* New York: Paulist Press, 1979.

Catherine of Siena: *Catherine of Siena: The Dialogue (The Classics of Western Spirituality).* New York: Paulist Press, 1980; Catherine M. Meade, *My Nature Is Fire.* Staten Island, New York: Alba House, 1991.

Charles Borromeo: *The Office of Readings.*

Charles de Foucauld: *Spiritual Autobiography of Charles de Foucauld.* Denville, New Jersey: Dimension Books, © 1964.

Claude de la Colombière: *Hearts on Fire: Praying with Jesuits.* St. Louis, Missouri: The Institute of Jesuit Sources, 1993; George Guitton, S.J., *Perfect Friend: The Life of Blessed Claude de la Colombière.* St. Louis, Missouri: B. Herder Book Co., © 1956.

Clement I: *The Office of Readings.*

Clement of Alexandria: *The Writings of the Fathers Down to A.D. 325.* The Anti-Nicene Fathers, Volume II; ed. Alexander Roberts and James Donaldson. Grand Rapids, Michigan: Wm. B. Eerdmans Publishing Company, 1987.

Columban: *The Office of Readings.*

Cyprian: *The Office of Readings.*

Cyril of Jerusalem: *The Office of Readings.*

Dominic: Father Thomas Plassmann, *Lives of Saints with Excerpts from Their Writings.* New York: John J. Crawley & Co., Inc., 1954.

Edith Stein: *The Collected Works of Edith Stein, Volume Two.* Washington, D.C.: ICS Publications, 1987.

Elizabeth of the Trinity: *The Complete Works, Volume Two.* Washington, D.C.: ICS Publications, 1995; *Sister Elizabeth of the Trinity: Spiritual Writings.* New York: P.J. Kennedy & Sons, 1962.

Elizabeth Seton: *Elizabeth Seton: Selected Writings.* Mahwah, New Jersey: Paulist Press, 1987.

Ephrem: *The Office of Readings.*

Faustina Kowalska: *Diary: Divine Mercy in My Soul.* Stockbridge, Massachusetts: Congregation of Marians of the Immaculate Conception, © 1987.

Fidelis of Sigmaringen: *The Office of Readings.*

Frances of Rome: Lady Georgiana Fullerton, *The Life of St. Frances of Rome.* New York: D. & J. Sadlier & Co.

Frances Xavier Cabrini: Enzo Lodi, *Saints of the Roman Calendar.* Staten Island, New York: Alba House, 1992; Segundo Galilea, *In Weakness, Strength: The Life and Missionary Activity of Saint Frances Xavier Cabrini.* New York: Missionary Sisters of the Sacred Heart of Jesus, 1996.

Francis de Sales: St. Francis de Sales, *Introduction to the Devout Life.* Garden City, New York: Doubleday Image Books, 1972; *The Office of Readings.*

Francis of Assisi: Regis J. Armstrong, *St. Francis of Assisi: Writings for a Gospel Life.* New York: The Crossroad Publishing Co., 1995.

Frederick Ozanam: The Vatican, www.vatican.va/holy_father/john_paul_ii/travels/documents/hf_jp_ii_hom_22081997_en.html.

Fulgentius of Ruspe: *The Office of Readings.*

Gabriel of the Sorrowful Mother: Rev. Charles Dolan, *Prayerbook of the Saints.* Huntington, Indiana: Our Sunday Visitor Press, 1984.

Gemma Galgani: Rev. Charles Dolan, *Prayerbook of the Saints.* Huntington, Indiana: Our Sunday Visitor Press, 1984.

Gerard Majella: Charles Dilgskron, C.S.S.R., *Life of Blessed Gerard Majella.* New York: The Redemptorist Fathers, 1892.

Gertrude: *The Office of Readings.*

Gianna Beretta Molla: *Love Letters to My Husband.* Boston, Massachusetts: Pauline Books & Media, 2002.

Gregory of Nazianzen: *The Office of Readings.*

Gregory of Nyssa: *The Office of Readings.*

Hilary: *The Office of Readings.*

Irenaeus: *The Office of Readings.*

Ignatius of Antioch: *The Office of Readings.*

Isaac Jogues: Lillian M. Fisher, *North American Martyrs: Jesuits in the New World.* Boston, Massachusetts: Pauline Books & Media, 1999.

Isaac of Stella: *The Office of Readings.*

Isaac of Syria: Robert Llewelyn, *The Joy of the Saints.* Springfield, Illinois: Templegate Publishers, 1992.

Isidore: *The Office of Readings.*

James Alberione: Quotes taken from unpublished writings, private archives of the Daughters of St. Paul.

Jane de Chantal: André Ravier, S.J., *Saint Jeanne de Chantal: Noble Lady, Holy Woman.* San Francisco: Ignatius Press, 1989; *The Office of Readings.*

Jeanne Jugan: Excerpt taken from the homily of Pope John Paul II on the occasion of her beatification.

Jerome: *The Office of Readings.*

John Berchmans: Albert S. Foley, S.J., *A Modern Galahad: St. John Berchmans.* Milwaukee, Wisconsin: The Bruce Publishing Company, © 1937.

John Bosco: Enzo Lodi, *Saints of the Roman Calendar.* Staten Island, New York: Alba House, 1992; *The Office of Readings.*

John Chrysostom: *The Office of Readings.*

John Climacus: *The Office of Readings.*

John Damascene: *The Office of Readings.*

John Eudes: *The Office of Readings.*

John Gabriel Perboyre: G. de Montgesty, *Two Vincentian Martyrs.* Maryknoll, New York: Catholic Foreign Mission Society of America, 1925.

John Mary Vianney: W.M.B., ed. *Thoughts of the Curé d'Ars.* Rockford, Illinois: TAN Books and Publishers, Inc., 1984.

John Neumann: *The Autobiography of John Neumann, C.S.S.R.* Boston, Massachusetts: Pauline Books & Media, 1977.

John of God: Enzo Lodi, *Saints of the Roman Calendar.* Staten Island, New York: Alba House, 1992; *The Office of Readings.*

John of Kanty: "Canon Law Resources." OpusBonaSacerdotii, www.opusbonosacerdotii.org/canon_law.htm

John of the Cross: *The Collected Works of St. John of the Cross.* Garden City, New York: Doubleday and Company, Inc., 1964.

John XXIII: Mario Benigni and Goffredo Zanchi, *John XXIII— The Official Biography.* Boston, Massachusetts: Pauline Books & Media, 2001.

Joseph Cafasso: St. John Bosco, *St. Joseph Cafasso, Priest of the Gallows.* Rockford, Illinois: TAN Books and Publishers, Inc., 1993.

Joseph Calasanz: *The Office of Readings.*

Joseph Moscati: Dr. Carmelita Laupus, "Life of Dr. Joseph Moscati" (paper given at the National Conference of Catholic Physicians Guild, November 1989).

Julie Billiart: Roseanne Murphy, S.N.D. de N., *Julie Billiart: Woman of Courage.* Mahwah, New Jersey: 1995.

Julian of Norwich: Juliana of Norwich, *Revelations of Divine Love.* Garden City, New York: Doubleday Image Books, 1977; Julian of Norwich, *Revelation of Love.* New York: Doubleday Image Books, 1996.

Katharine Drexel: Ellen Tarry, *Saint Katharine Drexel.* Boston, Massachusetts: Pauline Books & Media, 1999.

Lawrence Justinian: *The Office of Readings.*

Leo the Great: *The Office of Readings.*

Louis de Montfort: Peter John Cameron, O.P., *Classics of Catholic Spirituality.* Staten Island, New York: Alba House, 1996.

Louis Guanella: Megan McKenna, *The New Stations of the Cross: The Way of the Cross According to Scripture.* New York: Doubleday Image Books, 2003.

Louise de Marillac: M.V. Woodgate, *St. Louise de Marillac.* St. Louise, Missouri: B. Herder Book Co., 1946; *Vincent de Paul and Louise de Marillac: Rules, Conferences and Writings (The Classics of Western Spirituality).* New York: Paulist Press, 1995.

Madeleine Sophie Barat: Phil Kilroy, *Madeleine Sophie Barat: A Life.* Mahwah, New Jersey: Paulist Press, 2000; Maud Monahan, *Saint Madeleine Sophie.* New York: Longmans, Green & Co., 1925.

Margaret Mary Alacoque: *The Office of Readings.*

Marie of the Incarnation: *Marie of the Incarnation: Selected Writings (Sources of American Spirituality).* Mahwah, New Jersey: Paulist Press, 1989.

Mary Magdalene de Pazzi: *The Office of Readings.*

Maximilian Kolbe: Enzo Lodi, *Saints of the Roman Calendar.* Staten Island, New York: Alba House, 1992.

Maximus: *The Office of Readings.*

Patrick: John Healy, *The Life and Writings of Saint Patrick.* Dublin: M.H. Gill & Sons, 1905.

Paul Miki: Leonard Foley, O.F.M., revised by Pat McCloskey, O.F.M. *Saint of the Day.* Cincinnati, Ohio: St. Anthony Messenger Press, 1999.

Paul of the Cross: Martin Bialas, *The Mysticism of the Passion in St. Paul of the Cross.* San Francisco: Ignatius Press, © 1990; *The Office of Readings.*

Peter Chrysologus: *The Office of Readings.*

Peter Claver: *Hearts on Fire: Praying with Jesuits.* St. Louis, Missouri: The Institute of Jesuit Sources, 1993.

Peter Damian: *The Office of Readings.*

Peter Faber: *Hearts on Fire: Praying with Jesuits.* St. Louis, Missouri: The Institute of Jesuit Sources, 1993.

Peter of Alcantara: ThinkExist,www.thinkexist.com/English/Author/x/Author_4047_1.htm.

Philip Neri: *The Office of Readings.*

Pier-Giorgio Frassati: Luciana Frassati, *Man of the Beatitudes*. Slough, England: St. Paul Publications, 1990.

Pio of Pietrelcina: Don Mullan, *A Little Book of Padre Pio*. Boston, Massachusetts: Pauline Books & Media, 2003.

Piux X: F.A. Forbes, *Pope St. Pius X*. Rockford, Illinois: TAN Books & Publishers, Inc.; 1992.

Polycarp: Office of Readings.

Restituta Kafka: Alfred de Manche, "Blessed Restituta Kafka," http://jerome2007.tripod.com/ restituta_kafka.htm

Robert Bellarmine: *The Office of Readings.*

Rose of Lima: *The Office of Readings.*

Rose Philippine Duchesne: Catherine M. Mooney, R.S.C.J., *Philippine Duchesne: A Woman with the Poor.* Mahwah, New Jersey: Paulist Press, 1990.

Sophronius: *The Office of Readings.*

Stanislaus Kostka: Joseph E. Kearns, S.J., *Portrait of a Champion: A Life of St. Stanley Kostka.* Westminster, Maryland: The Newman Press, 1957.

Teresa of Avila: St. Teresa of Avila, *Interior Castle.* Garden City, New York: Doubleday Image Books, 1961; *The Office of Readings.*

Teresa of Calcutta: Malcolm Muggeridge, *Something Beautiful for God.* San Francisco: Harper San Francisco, 1986; Mother Teresa, *A Gift for God.* New York: HarperCollins, 1975.

Théophane Vénard: Christian Simmonnet, *Théophane Vénard: A Martyr of Vietnam.* San Francisco, Ignatius Press, 1988.

Theophilus of Antioch: *The Office of Readings.*

Theodore Guerin: Penny Blaker Mitchell, *Mother Theodore Guerin: A Woman for Our Time.* Saint Mary-of-the-Woods, Indiana: Sisters of Providence, © 1998.

Thérèse of Lisieux: St. Thérèse of Lisieux, *The Autobiography of St. Thérèse of Lisieux.* New York: Doubleday, 1957; *The Office of Readings;* SoultoSpirit, www.soultospirit.com/pgrow/subdirectory/life_purpose.asp.

Thomas Aquinas: *The Office of Readings.*

Thomas Becket: *The Office of Readings.*

Thomas More: *The Office of Readings.*

Thomas of Villanova: *The Lives of St. Thomas of Villanova and of St. Francis Solano.* London: Thomas Richardson and Son, 1947.

Timothy Giaccardo: Quotes taken from unpublished writings, private archives of the Daughters of St. Paul.

Vincent de Paul: *The Office of Readings.*

Vincent Ferrer: *The Office of Readings.*

Vincent Pallotti: Eugene Weber, S.A.C., *Vincent Pallotti: An Apostle and Mystic.* Staten Island, New York: Alba House, 1964.

William of Saint Thierry: *The Office of Readings.*

BOOKS & MEDIA

The Daughters of St. Paul operate book and media centers at the following addresses. Visit, call or write the one nearest you today, or find us on the World Wide Web, www.pauline.org

CALIFORNIA

3908 Sepulveda Blvd, Culver City, CA 90230 310-397-8676

5945 Balboa Avenue, San Diego, CA 92111 858-565-9181

46 Geary Street, San Francisco, CA 94108 415-781-5180

FLORIDA

145 S.W. 107th Avenue, Miami, FL 33174 305-559-6715

HAWAII

1143 Bishop Street, Honolulu, HI 96813 808-521-2731

Neighbor Islands call: 866-521-2731

ILLINOIS

172 North Michigan Avenue, Chicago, IL 60601 312-346-4228

LOUISIANA

4403 Veterans Memorial Blvd, Metairie, LA 70006 504-887-7631

MASSACHUSETTS

885 Providence Hwy, Dedham, MA 02026 781-326-5385

MISSOURI

9804 Watson Road, St. Louis, MO 63126 314-965-3512

NEW JERSEY

561 U.S. Route 1, Wick Plaza, Edison, NJ 08817 732-572-1200

NEW YORK

150 East 52nd Street, New York, NY 10022 212-754-1110

78 Fort Place, Staten Island, NY 10301 718-447-5071

PENNSYLVANIA

9171-A Roosevelt Blvd, Philadelphia, PA 19114 215-676-9494

SOUTH CAROLINA

243 King Street, Charleston, SC 29401 843-577-0175

TENNESSEE

4811 Poplar Avenue, Memphis, TN 38117 901-761-2987

TEXAS

114 Main Plaza, San Antonio, TX 78205 210-224-8101

VIRGINIA

1025 King Street, Alexandria, VA 22314 703-549-3806

CANADA

3022 Dufferin Street, Toronto, ON M6B 3T5 416-781-9131

¡También somos su fuente para libros, videos y música en español!